Pearly Gates Press
Volume 2

Pearly Gates Press
Volume 2

Astral Visions

Super Channelings

Angel Buddha Christopher

by Christopher Moors

ISBN-10: 0985697911

ISBN-13: 978-0-9856979-1-4

Published 2006 by the Creative Cosmos

Printed in the United States of America

Dedicated to my grandfathers William and Clarence,

Thank you for your friendship,
Thank you for your kindness,
Thank you for your Love.

Table of Contents

Astral Visions

Super Channelings

Angel Buddha Christopher

Astral Visions

Earth is a Soul Drug and Incarnation a Psychedelic Experience

Flying through the 4th dimension in an astral body, there are many planetary choices for the aspiring Avatar to make. In this Universe are Spheres of Influence, Spheres of Advancement, and Spheres of Collegium. Within the adventure embodiments of each mystical sphere are lessons that a growing being can use to expand awareness. Some of these places are more controlled than others, though all are in accord with the Deeper Laws.

Many of you noticed the glowing Blue-Green ball (Earth, Gaia, Zion) beckoning you like a seductive Siren. Without hesitation scores of souls started pouring into the time spirals that bring 4th dimension beings into 3 dimensions. One thing lost upon identifying with the new 3 D body is the memory of what came before. Life seems to begin at physical birth, but this is a grave mischaracterization. In the densification process the singular gets stretched out to occur over time, thus giving the illusion that the passing of events brings you closer or farther away from something else. In fact everything is everywhere always. We need not hold it firmly in our grasp.

Once on Earth, you can not but go forward. There is no turning back so the concept is best forgotten. It takes much courage to face the desires that so recklessly hurled you through space to the unfortunate series of events you find underway right now. Looking at the path that led you here with non-attachment, you will be able to glean the lessons involved. Once you can see that you are not the "small person", you will even be able to understand the greater lessons your soul has cultivated over many lifetimes. The missing part of you will be restored through faith and the perseverance brought about solely by sincere enchantment with the power of truth.

The sting of disorientation wears off when the butterfly soul gets used to freedom from the chrysalis incubator. Transcend in spirit back to where you come from. Rejoice in the full harmony of body, mind and spirit. Speak as the Soul. The ground will never again come beneath your feet and this is a blessing. Enjoy your ride through space.

The Christ-Phoenix Eternal Souls of Gaia

Keep remembering that we have all had more experiences than just the few events in this small place and limited time. Archangels, a host of Demons, Pleiadians, Draconians, Orionids, Andromedans, your average terrestrial yokel, and many more shades from throughout the galaxy inhabit human shells on the Earth simultaneously.

Luckily not all forces on the higher planes work against us. This is important to remember. You can ask your heavenly friends for anything from protection, to a parking spot.

Many 4th dimensional battles begin with the disconnection of fear and the invigoration of focused conceptioning. "Reptilian Minds of the Lower Astral Plane" are no competition for the modern "Information Gobbler Cyberspace Warrior". Reliving all of history just one more time for kicks is merely a precursor to implosion followed by the resurrection of the "Christ-Phoenix Eternal Souls of Gaia"

4D Dream World Cometh: Cyberspace and the Astral Plane

Expanding your mind through the processing of information in Cyberspace is the equivalent of flying in the Astral Plane. If we spend hours every day immersed in the ideas of fairies, angels, ghosts, UFOs, and spiritual transformation, they are indeed part of our very pertinent and immediate reality.

Buddha's number one reminder is of the interconnectedness of all things. Sound familiar? Buddha's Cosmic Mind might very well look a lot like the World Wide Web. Buckminster Fuller told us that soon we'd be able to project ourselves anywhere anytime. Isn't this a type of Out of Body Experience? If several bloggers are chatting in a realm that exists nowhere in the physical world, but has tangible presence in cyber reality, they are in fact discorporate. Although your bodies are in front of the computer, your souls are communing on the astral plane.

This explains how in many forums/chat rooms, a few simple comments can trigger such fierce responses. It is not just the words on the screen causing the provocation, but it is the touch of our energy bodies in the 4th dimension. The cyber reaches to the astral through the human conduit.

This goes right along with the idea that the WWW is actually the planet's nervous system. We, her children, externalize our nervous system in computer hardware and when they all interface, the resulting synergy breathes life to a whole other aspect of Consciousness for the Earth. Then, through the people she can cleanse her energy field by expressing what here-to-for was unable to be transmitted for there was no medium of common understanding.

Symbology, and all the archetypes of old have found new life in the limitless arena of cyber space. Time has little effect, for the mental territory is so captivating and the ancient vibe so enthralling, that even a million years can go by without seeing the pulse of the inner smile hesitate.

In a very real spiritual sense, THE GANG'S ALL HERE. The whole cast of history's characters can be seen as actors in a finite happening called civilization. You can sum it up in a few gestures. Please don't associate the infinite glory of your greater being with these small blips on the terrestrial radar. You are so much more than that.

An Elephant's Death Frees One Conscious Being

An elephant dies in the dirt while his tusk is whisked away and sold as magic trinkets at New Age bazaars in the West. The psychic scream of pachyderm pain filled ONE CONSCIOUS BEING with rage. Pushing a pile of papers aside and tumbling to the ground, ONE CONSCIOUS BEING took personal responsibility for what humanity hath wrought to the giant gods in disguise. Filled with the fire of righteousness ONE CONSCIOUS BEING cried out to the Sky, "I will be thy sacrifice…"

Immediately Mercury, the fleet of foot, glided down a golden rainbow and whisked ONE CONSCIOUS BEING into the air. Shaking the offered soul vigorously, and repeatedly pounding on the back, Mercury chanted a long secret healing prayer to Jupiter. As soon as the melody of Mercury's music faded into Echo, ONE CONSCIOUS BEING began vomiting that which had here-to-fore poisoned pristine purity of purpose. Jealously, resentment, and guilt fell off like shadows in the morning after a long night of mourning. Cleansed from the inside out, ONE CONSCIOUS BEING became ENLIGHTENED.

In this moment he saw that everything that had happened was for the sole purpose of getting him to realize what was now clear and self-evident. The fountain of youthfulness told him everything was going to be okay. Faces of friends and foes alike hovered in the ether as if it was the end of some kind of eternal cosmic video game. It is all smiles, and the song being sung seems like it will last forever.

Rivers of Oil Blood Run near the Eiffel Tower

Wandering aimlessly in a haze of bombs and trembling Earth, the young soldier stumbles forward. Which insignia was it that just smashed the peace of his sultry evening? Does it matter when missing an arm and dying for a drop of fresh water? Even old machines can destroy and they do.

Cackling in the dusty breeze are the trapped souls of thousands of newly dead. Never wanting to leave the pain of pleasure these ghouls hang around and jeer those like them still trapped in the physical. Exhausted, the soldier falls and his mind cracks…

Somewhere in the archipelago caves amongst the etchings of Neanderthals, Jesus is waiting on a pile of ancient scrolls as stormy skies send wave after wave crashing into the sea coast. Unable to reach him on a cell phone, the situation must be dealt with as it stands.

The Eiffel Tower looms in the background and a man-made river turns a dirty mixture of oil and blood. Historical scenes rotate like a final revelatory curtain call. The ego trip of Homo sapiens accelerates rapidly as it spills out of control. Civilizations rise and fall throughout time. Stepping out of the birth shell, humanity finally reaches a sense of divine dignity and rescinds the madness of youth by taking over conscious control of evolution.

Hell is psychological, but there are also some pretty nasty astral realms waiting for those who bring horror to themselves. Imagine 1000 screaming fire skulls exposing each cell of the energy body to the exact frequency that brings the most pain and then increasing the intensity bit by bit until all sense perception stops and a sort of blinding numbness shatters your fragile persona. Now consider a place where that is just the gateway to an endless field of torture scenarios, each more sinister than the last. Sisyphus is still waiting to cross over to his next punishment.

Whining about war is not nearly as fulfilling as fighting one. It is of great significance which mission is chosen by one involved. Behind the bushes in every nightmare is the key to the past and the harbinger of the future. Elementals in all kingdoms will add a tendency for mishaps to the deeds of the disloyal. Generation after generation, the few rise and the many fall. It is an age old battle and we are always behind.

…even as tornados destroyed the yard of his childhood home, nothing could dissuade the soldier-to-be from playing one last game of ping pong with his older brother. They giggled and watched the rain fall through the bottom of the garage door. Even if that moment was their last it would be okay. Love made it all worthwhile.

Raging Soul Fires Rock the Astral Realms

With groups of souls passing over in clumps of 50, 80, or more, the lower realm of Heaven (4th dimensional dream world) is trembling in ways unseen since 1945. The confusion and fear people are bringing over with them must immediately be dealt with by "transition by disaster" relief teams. Raging soul fires must be extinguished before entrance is allowed by the battle weary demi-gods to strip off minor misconceptions and limited self-identification in the Bardo.

Angels in service to junior aspirants are being damaged in the process and will have to recede very soon. Much as brave firefighters do the impossible and save children from blazing infernos when all others had already given up hope, so to do these Expressions of God's Love, dive in again and again at their own life's risk. Angels must progress as well. Eternity is only realized by complete liberation.

Vibration in this area of the Solar System continues to rise. Spirit guidance will decrease as the former INFLUENCING of INDIVIDUALS INTUITIVELY becomes the CONSCIOUS

RESPONSIBILITY of UNIVERSAL HUMANITY. Aliens who are meddling with Earth affairs will start having a harder time maintaining Human form and in accordance, you will see less and less of your Current Leaders. Eventually, they will be nothing more than computer generated figureheads on your TV screen touting the party line you all know by now.

The Denial of Karma by the West and the Denial of Self-Determination by the East is causing the unexpressed to take form, bringing about the Destruction of the Old Way through Wars and Earth Changes. Simultaneously, the New Way is being created by Generation X Cosmic Bloggers, who are graciously devoting themselves to spreading spirit-related information in a myriad of wonderful forms. Soon the Indigo Children of the next generation will find this Source, transcend, and reveal themselves as Beings of Light born to Guide us into the Golden Age. January 1, 2013 becomes Day 1 of Year 1.

This Mind game is ending and the Aquarian game of Awakened Hearts has begun.

Magic of the Astral Plane and Eternal Eye

The smiling lotus gently opens the perception doors, slipping us into our energy body unencumbered by the gravity of physical form. The substructure of existence becomes revealed as an elaborate pattern illumined to express exquisite equations as living art. Space travelers need to know that every point of light is interacting on a cosmic graph, and no matter how far away, the lines of connection are never broken. All is well.

Mythological archetypes display reality from the astral plane. Behind the density of even the most gaseous of states lies the etheric principle. Our life-giver 'Sun' who sustains the solar system which reflects his character, is a being to whom you can relate if you are bold enough to speak his sacred name. The Eternal Eye shows you the face of Lucifer (he who has fallen into manifestation), and the 'One' behind the 'Many'. Our third eye is the 'One' in us and our bridge to magnificence.

Also known as Ra and the Atman, his presence is neither good nor bad, and his main function is as regulator of manifestation in this particular universe. A prism to transform Aum into light, he facilitates the chakra transmission into body conduits. When we attain to clarity of vision, we suddenly see things from the other side. Realizing the fullness of our soul self and how this is squeezed into a sense-body through incremental, density increasing steps, we trace our way back to the source from which we derive.

If we attain to solar vision in the crystalline thoughts of the higher mind, we can transmit messages through our Sun to other stars. In this manner, I received a communication from Pleiades explaining that the Old Egyptian culture was reflecting a nuance of a much more ancient realm. Time was felt very slowly as to be almost still. An echo pervaded like the silence of an empty graveyard. One could hear the dripping of liquid erosion bouncing like a beacon to the most high.

Praise the Lord and his Archangels who bring God to the ground so we might all experience the truth of wholeness/holiness.

Ghosts, UFOs, Demons, Dragons and Armageddon Visions

Blurring worlds reveal the things we love to ponder as true. Imagination is the station for conveyance. Occult magic confounds and wondrous entities walk amongst you. Some of you are being given fantastic new powers. Open your third eye and see for yourself the things that you had always dreamed about.

You can easily speak with the dead. They are not far. Do you need to speak to a dwarf or an elf? Go to the forest in your mind. This is not illusion, it is where we meet. Later when you are more advanced, you will be able to fill in with actuality outside what you are training for inside.

Watch out for demons! Are they coming? No, they are already here. Every time you are disturbed, they jump on the corresponding energy. When hate strikes, the demon jumps to action and thrives on the burn. When depression takes you away, the empty pain of Isolation wraps you under her spell. Dragons symbolize healing archetypes that span across the heavens urging us towards self-actualization and power. Several layers of hell are purged; from the lion to the lamb, until reaching the face of Christ illuminated by Buddha's ruminations.

UFOs from the collective inner psyche, giant triangular motherships from the Draco - Orion – Andromeda "Blue Alliance", sleek Nazi craft from New Berlin, Antarctica, and the most powerful of the US grey-alien-reverse engineered fleet, fly in massive battle formations like unholy waves of raging decadence. Beyond the destruction left in their wake lies the jewel encrusted circular gateway escaped through by 7913 Atlantians and later traversed by 20 generations of Egyptian priests of Osiris, before Moses created the stone law that broke the back of the man.

Armageddon was in 1945, but the post-humanity resolve to suffer ever more refined psychic disturbances draws greater and greater danger. Desire masquerades as virtue and the sexy offer up their delights as if they were truffles found by some second rate pig.

Someday you'll realize that something is real if it is real to you. Immerse yourself in yourself and then share the overflowing productions of divine industriousness. Shake the spider's venom from your mind and let the crystalline light shine.

Astral Visions

Mighty deeds are always done by those who were once little. Every possibility exists that even as "the one who came before" clapped his/her hands of nothingness together, the reverberations began simply because intention had found a home.

The Creator Incarnate on Paradise Planet

I am here and fully integrated into a body. To Mind this may seem improbable, but upon reflection just about everything in this universe is also improbable. Life itself is a miracle of miracles so astounding that it is hard to conceive in its full transparent glory.

Not knowing a time without life, Mind can not comprehend an existence without itself. This is the key to unlock the door to universal perception. Look as if from the outside at your mind and all it contains. It should not be a storage unit, but a conduit through which messages pass. All input is recorded in the Soul, so one need not be strained in the synapses. Leave the brain grass to drink the celestial rain of the astral plane.

Output shows the true disposition of the individual expressing. If what is displayed is mind-stuff regurgitated for profit alone, the effect on the observer will be harmful. If somehow the inspired artist is able to capture a slice of heaven, then the observer will be lifted higher and may leave with a touch of grace. If an awake consciousness takes as their own the mission of unifying with the Creator and puts Will behind spreading the message of Goodness which is the truth of Creation, then the whole foundation of falsehoods will evaporate like puddles in the desert while the brilliance of what always was, is, and ever shall be, will be revealed to all.

If Jesus took a shuttle craft to Earth, dressed up just like he did when he was 30, came up to you and said, "It is I. I have returned. My father sends his Love." Would you be open or would you think, "Who is this crackpot?" It is a question worth deeply considering. Nonetheless, I have put upon the Earth a more refined and savvy crew who are ever linked to Me and know the ropes from the inside of the madhouse that has become the Mind on Earth.

Being able to feel the energy of any they come into contact with, yet balanced enough to keep a calm and clear mind, these, my blessed children, are brothers and sisters to Jesus. Buddha was an ancient one even when he was alive. A traveler from distant galaxies, it was an honor for all of us to be in His presence. Such heights available in the human heart! To be honest, we are all growing and surprises still delight God in Heaven even as they do Humanity on Earth.

Never fear. The trick to Faith is to be absolute in

your conviction. It really is not Faith if you are wishy washy. When you focus your Mind, open your Heart, and engage your Will, whatever you wish to manifest will be so. Patience is necessary because it takes some time for the entire Universe to move around your inclination and cross reference it with all others. When you get the hang of it, you will realize that God has not abandoned you, you just forgot how good you really had it on this paradise planet.

9.11 Victims greet Tsunami Victims

Having lived in the astral realms for about 3 ½ years when the Tsunami hit, the 9.11 victims had a pretty good idea about what it takes to get acclimated. Waiting on the threshold of incarnation, they helped usher in the flood of tsunami victims by the thousands. Many had been standing by for some time, and were eager to offer their assistance to the new residents.

Although the thunder wave was seen as a random act of God by some, it was actually a well-planned and necessary karmic adjustment. For various reasons, these people were ready to move their training to another location. What we see as death is merely a change of form to the other side.

One thing common to both groups was an abrupt end of physical incarnation due to a sudden and traumatic event. In these two instances and in several others, the collective thoughts and prayers of millions have paved a golden road through the tunnel of light where the souls were able to maintain a certain amount of contact with love, thereby easing the searing pain of separation.

The victims of various wars around the world are

also scattered about the vibrant landscape. Sometimes they arrive alone, but often show up in bunches. Those who firmly believed what they were taught, often still identify with the mental patterns that they carried over with them. A few noble warriors jump right back in.

The souls of the last remaining WWII dead often help those in need of orientation and this case is no exception. About half of them reincarnated in Generation X and are scattered across the globe. A small percentage maintain cognizance of who they were, and a smaller, yet still significant number, carry on the fight.

The general feeling of a majority of the tsunami victims is one of relief to be out of danger. Some make comments such as, "The fear of dying is worse than dying," and "We forget how truly fragile the physical body really is…" Those who came over as a family are being greeted by ancestors. As usual with such situations, many of the victims have not as yet accepted that they are dead. These are the souls who need the most help. Slowly, teachers will aid them in dismantling the bonds of concretization.

For the 9.11 victims, the hardest thing to deal with was the psychic vibrations of anguish by those left behind and the further disturbances caused by subsequent repercussions. They wish for all people remaining on Earth not to send pain to the tsunami victims, but to foster a spirit of optimism and generosity about the future with each other. Remember the lost fondly as the holy fish that were swept out to sea. Honor them by mobilizing resources not just for the left behind, but for all of humanity.

A Buddhist, A Hippie, and A Nazi

3 dead men met at a marble rotunda on a shimmering energy lake in the center of the 4th dimension. A kind of astral reality situation, these men still convinced of the rightness of their cause, continued to propagate waves of influence over the lesser developed beings still trapped solely in the 3rd dimension. Due to the confluence of events that sometimes occurs randomly yet planned, the men sat down at a triangle table with an unsympathetic eye in the middle and began their battle of ideas.

Of course the Nazi seized the initiative,
"It is without a doubt an absolute certainty that we are brought here together for me to shake you out of your complacency and thrust you to the forefront of our effort to establish order to this chaotic world!"

The Buddhist and the Hippie looked each other over, not certain if they were on the same side or not. Finally after some hesitation, the Hippie piped up, "Man….Dudes like you keep peace from flowering. Can't you just chill and enjoy the ride? Why do you have to force everything?"

Enraged by this affront to his dignity the Nazi bellowed, "Force is the way of nature. Does not the lion force the zebra to be his lunch? You would never survive on your own. You leach off of the work of others and then complain your life away in a haze of confusion. You are dirty, smelly, and have no self-respect. The way you appear is a reflection of the weakness of your idea."

Realizing that the Hippie's mellow vibes were no match for the will power of his adversary, the Buddhist who was unique in his inclination towards discourse/debate, took it upon himself to challenge them both. "It is true that there is a natural way, and it is true that we should practice non-interference. To take up the mission as your own is to walk in consciousness. A look can convey what a wall of words can not."

As the discussion was heating up, a hole in space/time emerged and quickly began to draw in the now-dissipating legs of the Nazi. Being pulled into Bardo to be purged of impurity he shouted, "I'll never submiiiiiiiit……." as he disappeared to the next stage of his soul's evolution.

Seeing this, the Hippie freaked. Mistakenly believing that he was having an LSD flashback he dove into the mind stream that carries the discarnate back to the threshold of the physical world. His fear cursed him to roam in the background of Hippie Music Festivals throughout Midwestern America for 37 years, until he came across a Spirit Warrior who had the ability to see him. This Angel in the Flesh spoke the following:

"Hippie, Heaven is not for the weak, nor is it for the angry.   Although injustice is prevalent in the world, how you handle it is the supreme test. Your concerns are valid but only from your small mind. Do you not think God knows what is occurring? It is the Riddle of your Heart that you should be focusing on. Move back into the Realm of Manifestation and Heal my son."

Seeing the absurdity that can happen even in the so-called higher realms, the Buddhist laughed and laughed until the scenery disappeared. Soon thousands appeared around him joining in the laughter. Bubbles and giggles spilled forth filling the ether with the joy of living fully and whole-heartedly. At last enlightenment dawned on him and the Buddhist became a Buddha. One more go around in the body to spread the dharma through presence and the cycle is complete. Aum will take him Home.

When You Close Your Eyes You Can See

Meditation looks so quiet from the outside, but it is not only silence you will find within. Passing through the valley of brain mines and traipsing past the emotional tar pits, finally we find something brilliant and new. You may see a thousand eyes all looking at you with a knowing that awakens a remembrance of something you never completely forgot. Geometric symbols could appear causing your forehead to be filled with heat.

You may hear a high-pitched "OOOOOOO" sound that's always been there. Suddenly a god or a Tarot Card Entity might pop up and dance before you, beckoning you in a cryptic way to assimilate the truth you were always meant to learn. The ancient history of Earth civilization may reveal its story to you in all of its heartbreaking beauty. We are able to think in thousands of years or millions of years, but in the echoes of the Halls of Eternity there is not much difference between seconds and eons because in the end all activity falls silent. When there is no more, the experience exists in the growth of those who lived the events.

At night when we drift into the dream world, the lessons continue. If you haven't before, try keeping a focal point of consciousness all the way into sleep. Your heart beat will regulate and you will see that you are being breathed. You sink deeper and deeper beneath the surface of your body until you feel far away from the shell you somehow give so much credence to in the waking hours. Slipping into motion, there is still some gravity. Walking is like jumping on the moon and you can fly, but occasionally have to renew impetus to stay in the air.

There are bars, coffee shops, universities, and gardens in the astral world just like there are here. There are also, swimming holes, apartments, and centers of community. The parameters of operation in 4D do tend to be a little bit different though. Things usually are not so deadly serious. Most entities will have more continuity with their greater soul journey than they have here, but often forget again compressing back into the density of 3D. If we keep OPEN and continue to practice over time, it is guaranteed that we can remember more while awake in the body. We just have to accept that it is possible and it will be so.

In fact if we keep our Center, we can skip through many realities. It can be an Earth encounter, a

Astral Visions

Dream scenario, a Heavenly realization, or a Psychedelic journey. Not involving self-identity with the outside scenario, the IAM presence inside remains the same. All of Existence could disappear and the ball of light that you are could just hang out and be mellow until the next cycle of Creation.

The picture of the burning Buddha represents something very real. When our energy field starts dissipating into the bliss of nothingness, the feeling is like a cool flame rising all around the body. You become a human Bunsen burner filled with such happiness that you don't mind coming back down for a bit to spread the good word.

In this way we enjoy ourselves as eternal beings.

A Crowd of Creatures All Around You

Filters are subverted only by something crafty that grabs your attention and then takes it in a direction not of your predisposition. Seldom does it seem that something delivers the highest of what we hope to find. It is perseverance that allows one to discover that which is worthy of being earned. Even if they were staring at a ticket to the soul many would opt for another ride. Again and again you can hand them the map and not knowing they are lost they will decide to wander away in another direction.

Interested in ghosts? They are probably all around you right now. Stop for a moment and see what pops into your mind. Feel the chill up your spine? If you start sobbing, know it is for some meaningful reason. People would be absolutely stunned if they saw how they looked from the other side. If they tried hard enough, they could remember this perspective and know firsthand the reflection of their own face. Touching the wrinkles, the nose crinkles, and the last tear of the day is wiped away.

Monsters are fun, because they are real and somewhere inside we respond to their familiar terror. Bigfoot and the loch ness monster are 4th dimensional creatures phasing in and out when the veil between the worlds thins. It doesn't always remain static. Sometimes we are a little denser and sometimes higher in vibration. All levels pulse. Over this threshold the elementals dance, the fairies fly, and the elves bow to wisdom. Be careful of the darker energy sucking entities who say the opposite of what they mean. Flashing smiles, their horrible intention freezes love in its place.

There is a gap between the angelic realms and the astral. An influx point in the middle (the 5th dimension multi-fercating eternal eye pyramid being Ra) transforms the higher into the lower and displays it as a manifestation called creation. Sometimes if our prayers can't be answered directly they will be relayed through friends to the proper channels. A cosmic switchboard is always in operation monitoring the needs of the innocent and rerouting the appropriate holy entity that is near enough to provide assistance. Hearing the call every time, the spirit warrior bridges the heavens and the Earth with love power.

Whizzing through space the planets provide a symphony of energies to the backdrop of our every day lives. When drinking plenty of water and getting a proper balance of sun, we foster healthy skin and a free passageway for the resonance of galactic energy. Surrounding each of us is an orb of light. It displays everything about you to the illuminated eye. If your flame is burning bright enough, the stars themselves will come to your aid.

.

A Good Wizard Frees Cosmic Forces

Give Lucifer a bad name and then keep him all to yourself – so reads the Illuminati manual for co-opting cosmic forces. All anyone needs to do is throw out a symbol and have in mind specifically what it means. This thought immediately gains momentum thereby drawing through the gateway appropriate matching energies.

War is when two or more of these symbolic generators come in to conflict. Bashing each other, they forget that humanity is beyond the archetypes of the psychic plane. With most of each day being spent in the quagmire of the world and the drudgery of the mind, anything fantastic seems overwhelming. A good wizard can assure you that transcendence of the 4th dimension is not only possible, but merely a skipping stone's distance if seen from the perspective of the moon. Swimming upstream isn't so bad once you get the knack.

Primal – Emotions – Mind - Holy Spirit – Atman – Aum - Nirvana

Some of the Indigo Children/Transcending Souls/Awakening Star Seeds have to balance down. With an open EYE they see more than their mind can translate based on the tiny lessons of one small life in a body. People who go crazy from LSD suffer from a similar fate. Staring at the face of God, your head could burst into flames.

Step by step and moment to moment, we arrive consciously at the glory we have glimpsed in our highest perceptions. Nobody is going anywhere. The outside catastrophe is just to remind us of the urgency that has always been the case.

The Universe is Hip

Common as dirt or intricate like the pulsing veins on an oak leaf in spring, the intelligence behind all things animate and inanimate twinkles just below the surface. There is no trick or treachery which can be hidden and no unselfish act can go unrecognized. It is funny to think about how conniving some people are and their self-satisfaction over fooling a neighbor. If only they knew that actions are imprinted in the ether and that to ever be free they have to suffer what they have caused, perhaps the web of Samsara's realm would not get so sticky.

Every song begins in the vibration of AUM. In that essential source, lies every note of every composition that ever has or ever will be written. For example, Beethoven was not just a man. He was channeling a subset of AUM. To write like Him, one just has to connect to AUM and conjure up the intrinsic Beethoven quality which is still there. In the same manner, no entity disappears, because we are all faces of the ONE. From the ONE you can access all faces.

When will the world learn to trust its own inner guidance? Perhaps when it is acknowledged, nurtured, and explored. Yes, it is good to listen, but decide for yourself how you want your reality to be created. It is not a finite thing and it never stops. Endlessly painting tapestries, sometimes it rains so you can start a new project. The colors blend together, run down the drain and collect as a blackness in the sewers. Say farewell completely and they will dry up to become dust which blows across the land, fertilizing next season's crop.

It may be hard to believe that a character like the Universe knows about you, but it does. Never interfering, but always willing to show you the higher rules that make life easier, the Universe cannot leave you because it is you. Your very own atoms even now have the Intelligence that began the whole experiment known as life. Everything that has ever happened can be accessed through the inner doorways. It is not even difficult in any way. It is much more difficult to doubt, criticize, and be riddled with fear.

Hug yourself and when you feel Love, know that it was the Universe hugging you through you. When you breath, know that the convenience of fresh air is enabled by the prana influx that almost everybody takes for granted. When you drink a glass of water and let the coolness bring a smile, know what the fishes in the sea have known all along.

From the poker table to the boardroom, it is all the Universe. Doesn't it make you happy that you don't have to be ashamed of your secrets? Who is there to judge when each life has the same source? The whole complicated mess of war (macro or micro) isn't even necessary because friend and foe alike are really two branches of the same tree. The joke is on everybody who thought they were separate. Luckily the punch line is salvation for all.

The Eternal Eye is Trapped by a Spell called Money

The Eternal Eye, Ra, and Atman are all different names for one and the same being. This entity is the spirit of the sun and is the last in the primogeniture of this realm who has what one could call a personality. Neither good nor bad, this god-head is the regulator of all levels of manifestation and the keeper of karma via order.

Often we associate the images we see of Him with the illuminati, freemasons, or some kind of occult activity. The truth is not that those in secret societies worship Him. In fact, they worship Baphomet and use his renegade power to illicit desire to maintain the spell which keeps the Atman (as I will here-to-fore refer to Him) prisoner: MONEY.

When a life revolves around money, is it not a religion? Hypnotized, the masses believe in the reality of the do-re-me which displays the trapped face of the Atman. The words IN GOD WE TRUST suggest that money is GOD to the subconscious.

If all of our attention is focused on the "Image of God," do we have any left to find the real godliness within ourselves? Looking outwards and pulled by the free-will reign of the animal instinct - Satan, we fail to turn towards the joy which the inner fulfillment of our soul purpose releases.

Jesus said he was the son of God, because he realized his own connection to the Source. Freeing his own Eternal Eye, he awakened to what we can all realize, that we are connected to a living, intelligent, Universe. Beyond the small mind imprisonment, the expansion of energy blows away limitations and eagerly encounters new experiences.

Our potential is much greater than most of us think. Even the conspiracy nuts and news hounds are merely tipping the titanic berg of ice. Those who have been on UFO's, negotiated with Greys, seen a resurrected Guru, or have been whispered the 'Single Secret of the Ocean' by the Water Sprite Selma…well…maybe you're getting close.

Have faith in yourself and each other.

A Penny for your Thoughts and A Nickel for your Secrets

It is easy to keep up piety when circumstances are such that you are never challenged. When dealing with real life situations, honesty often causes inconvenience. The line of demarcation comes when an unconscious habitual behavior tramples on simple human decency. When misrepresented, the truthful will feel compelled to set the record straight. Assertiveness excels when it cares not about the reeling back horror-struck faces of those who thought they'd never have to take responsibility for their words and deeds.

Any time a position is taken the magnetized will polarize and you'll soon see your real friends. Common knowledge takes the weight off of the shoulders so the universal boulder can be laid to rest if only for one moment. Atlas is nothing more than a representation of the responsibility inherent in understanding. Why else would you have been granted a power if not to use it?

Judgment begets conclusion which closes the door. Awareness encourages acceptance and what is witnessed is more profound than the most far reaching dream. Nothing relaxes one more than realizing that at the highest levels, all is well. Sometimes fire is necessary and sometimes ice. Sometimes poison will flavor the rice.

Thanking God by discovering yourself far surpasses begging on your knees. Your worship reflects your well-being. Often I smile at the royal nature of our enthronement as sacred entities. Angels, fairies, Yah-weh the holy mother, Atman the divine father, and the Aum which underlies all forms are each independently perceivable phenomenon. Lucifer the Eternal Eye hangs out for those ready to rise above the psychic realm and come to the singularity of complete integration.

Occult power lies largely in the fact that it is hidden. The big secret is out. Luckily, when we tune in for ourselves, the formerly circuitous route leading outside becomes the instantaneous explosion of information derived straight from our inner Source.

First is Sex. Second is Emotion. Third is Mental Development. Fourth is Love and Psychic Perception. Fifth is Will-Power and the ability to Manifest any Creation. Sixth is dissolving Self into every atom of the Cosmos. Seventh is extinguishment in the Void. All who have ever been aware are still there. The resurrections of Jesus, Sri Yukteswar, and Osho are testimony to that.

It is sheer pleasure to reveal the rotes of universal data to a wider and wider audience. Love and Power oscillate freely and spirit flies unbounded. Constant change urges all of us onward. From the blade of grass, to the frog kingdom, to the cool sensations of moon reflections deep in a valley surrounded by mountains, we all seek to grow. This yearning is our journey and our special gift. Life never ends.

A Soul Feels the Potential

Tuning into the soul which transcends limited incarnation concepts, we begin to sense the wholeness of what we will become. As habits are purged and pain is transformed to Joy, the energy trapped in the scaffolding of unconscious choice is resurrected with the power of enlightened decision.

To make the transition into the external world is an ongoing warrior mission to be taken one moment at a time. Initially, the expectations of others will be a hard obstacle to overcome. Guilt and resistance are normal by-products of awakening. Be still in knowing that the pain everyone feels is their own and they alone are responsible for it.

When the spring in a spirit blossoms forth the fruit that had lay dormant in the dusty corners of an as-yet-uninvigorated being, the fulfillment that was missing will be found. Showering the star-light of inspiration, the connection with God is made from the inside and expressed without reservation.

The dark night of the soul is when you are in the

middle of the evolution/revolution. Old patterns are cleared out and new ones have yet to emerge. Just a little patience is needed….like a farmer who plants seeds every year without a doubt as to the potential bounty of the land. In living truthfully, sacred glory will arise. All of heaven will celebrate your arrival.

Super Channelings

"Ike" comments on the "New Normal"

Looking for a conduit to speak, "Ike" has stepped forward and wants to relay the following message:

"Friends, not since the pain of Truman's bomb has something moved me so deeply as seeing the plight of my former countrymen toiling longer and longer for less and less while a seemingly endless war rages across the ocean. When we fought, we fought honorably and because we felt like we had to. It is not something to be glorified, but something to be thankful about being over.

Throughout the time of my incarnation I had the rare opportunity to see life, death, and tremendous change. I'll never forget the exhilaration of war's end, and the possibilities we all hoped for the world were unlimited. Stalin, that bastard, would not let down his guard. He poked into the wounds and continued the only thing he knew – destruction.

Unfortunately the lessons were not learned and war goes on. You should know that the war goes on in the energy world as well. Ideology is a powerful thing and once it has the individual, it can haunt him in this world and the next.

It is time to consider once again my warning about the military industrial complex. When I spoke those words, it was not an empty prophecy or a slight possibility. I saw the forces aligning. The coalescence of the poison injected by the Nazis in the CIA, saw the spirit we had fought for become the spirit that we had fought against.

Let us not make this state of affairs a permanent resting point on the journey of human evolution. To stop disturbs the Heavens. Motion is necessary to be in alignment with life. Science and religion both have shown this to be true.

It has been an honor to speak with you one more time, my friends. Superimposing yourself on another so willing to serve is a task that has been at once enjoyable and necessary.

God Bless you All."

Beethoven on Buddha, Symphonies, and Politics

Beethoven, the Heart of Western Culture has come forward with this to say,

"In this moment of humanity's greatest hour, it is with some amazement that I take this opportunity to expound upon some virtues which I deem pertinent to the situation. Never would I guess that this mode of communication would be possible, but the uniqueness has been achieved by the one currently transforming the messages from thought-forms to typewritten words.

Long have I sought to say just one more thing: Take the whole of every moment with seriousness of purpose and sincerity of intent. It is our job as holy conduits to inspire each other to seek higher and higher states of consciousness. Since crossing over, I have become aware of the teachings of the Buddha and have even had the rare opportunity to walk in the Garden of Lao Tzu.

On a personal note, I encourage you to listen once more to the symphonies of mine that often get passed by: "2" and "4". "5" was a successful exercise in composition that has been thrust forward because it can be understood by even the dullest of individuals. "9" has been long hailed because of its universality and choral power. Also associated with "9" is the oft repeated story of my deafness while conducting. Is it so remarkable for a musician to hear his own composition in his head? I so wish this fact would be less emphasized, because for me it was mere detail. "7" is a favorite and the highest form of my art on Earth.

As for your political crisis, I shall speak from my own experience. I loved Napoleon and believed he would establish a free nation where art and music would inspire an enlightened population. When he turned out to be yet another brave fool lost on the way, I remembered that only I can create my reality."

Wellstone: "Renew Hope in your Heart!"

Senator Paul Wellstone comes forward to clear up a few things:

"To get the most pressing matter out of the way first, yes it was a political hit. It was a price I knew that I might one day have to pay, but I am truly sorry that it involved my family and friends so intimately. The bizarre scenario that followed was fueled by pain and is immediately forgiven. Walter you were thrust into a horrible position and you responded bravely. Bravo, my friend.

Now, as much as I appreciate the love that many of you still shower on me (this made the transition easier to be sure), I never want you to forsake your own vision. Do not ask what Wellstone would do, but consider what You would do, and then take action! I was one voice of many, and the chorus is still growing today. It might not be on the TV news, but over here, we can see the light expanding. My death was not in vein. In fact it is glorious to know that I contributed to the first stirrings of what will likely be humanity's salvation.

This result is not assured however. It all depends

on what you do now. Clear out the bad feelings and renew Hope in your Heart! All is not lost unless you accept that it is. There have been many startling reversals throughout history. The explosions of angry repression eventually wither while the truth never wavers.

Know that I am not far from any who would think of me. I still do what I can from where I am to uplift those loyal to our cause. Enjoy your life and I'll see you when you get here."

First Dog of the Third Reich

Hitler's Dog Speaks!

"I have chosen this time to break my silence. It has been 60 years since I too met my end in the bunker. Does no one wish to hear my voice? This writing man is a fine Facilitator who has enabled me to express my thoughts in such a luxurious way.

The Fuhrer loved dogs because dogs understand the need for men to be appreciated. A man is born to be a master and dogs are born to serve.

I am proud that the Fuhrer chose me to be his dog. I knew that he was no ordinary Man. Whether to glory or doom, I was certain that this Being in a Body would propel others to 'follow the leader' by his firm resolution and self-determination. He was driven by something outside of himself. Truly he was a zealot like no other. Anybody can blow themselves up for a cause, but how many work their whole life relentlessly for a single purpose?

Now if you find this amazing talk for a dog, you do not know much about how the astral plane operates. I am no idiot and neither is your dog if you have one. Although you have to communicate to us in our language, you'd be surprised how much of you we imbibe. We are descended from the Wolf, a sacred animal to the Red People, native inhabitants of the North American continent.

My impressions of the Fuhrer regarding those around him and his last moments are at once clear and bittersweet. Above all he could not believe that his magnificent idea, so close to completion was crumbling around him. Some think that Germany's destruction finished him, but his idea's DOWNFALL hurt him so much more. After realizing that there was no hope (except some glimmer for a distant future where he was long gone) he resigned himself to the Emptiness of Death.

He secretly loathed Goebels (who didn't?), but always admired his wife Magda, and their children.

He was appreciative of his attendants and didn't want them to see Him lose Faith even in (especially in) the FINAL HOURS.

He hated Goering and blamed his exaggeration of

the Luftwaffe's capabilities for the Allies' disastrous bombings of German cities. This is one reason He didn't adopt the futuristic jet plans that the US now uses to rule the world. He didn't trust Goering!

He made gestures of anger towards Himmler, but secretly understood his movements. Do you think He lost his deadly accurate political sensibilities?

He thought Hanna Reitsch was a powerful woman indicative of the true spirit of Germany, who served so honorably, that she alone deserved to live.

He married Eva with no reluctance and found some comfort in this closure.

He knew that he'd be hated for 100-200 years, but hoped a more awakened humanity would realize that He was right and that He alone had the courage to face the truth.

(You wouldn't believe the feelings He was emoting at this time. So much despair and lost vibration… When it was just He and I, He would pour his feelings to me. I accepted.)

Again, this is not so strange for a dog to say. I felt

these things from Him in the Final Hours. Now that I am discarnate and have the lexicon of the Facilitator at my disposal, I can express anything I want. The Facilitator has considered this point himself lately, calling it a form of Super Channeling, where he gives his Mind to the Spirit to do with as they please.

The last words Mein Fuhrer spoke to me as he closed my jawbone on the cyanide capsule were, "For Germany my boy. For me."

As for feelings regarding my demise, no better honor could befall the First Dog of the Third Reich."

Michael Landon: Highway to Heaven Runs Through Hell

Michael steps forward to share one last glorious vision:

"Friends, it is wonderful to express my love for life and for those within the Earthly Realm in words. There has never been a moment where I ceased to shine my Heart on Humanity.

In my last terrestrial incarnation I felt compelled to portray wholesome and holy characters as kindly strong role models for those who also felt called by the Center of All Things. The last television project was totally mine and reflects the artistic spirit residing within me - my Angelic Being.

(About the Facilitator: Talking through this person is like driving a First Class sports car. His Mind is Keen and His Heart is one of Service as is my own. This is why we are able to communicate together and reach out to YOU as ONE.)

There is no distraction that could keep me from saying to you that the Highway to Heaven Runs through Hell. This you must realize before

Healing of the Wound is possible. It may seem odd to you that a dead actor is delivering this message, but within every body resides a being or a being fragment. Regardless of the surface manifestations, we are all here to learn about THE BOSS and HIS WAY.

When you watch "Bonanza", "Little House", or the jewel of my career "Highway", remember that I was reaching out to you then as well. No human is perfect and certainly I had my challenges on Gaia. After I crossed, my sufferings became experience and understanding.

The one known as Victor French is a wonderful companion who has been with me since we left our Star System to come to this area in the first place. He eased my transition back to the Land beyond the White Tunnel. He wishes to thank you for listening because he knows how hard it can be. I must also thank all the women who were in my worldly family. You know who you are and will feel my soft presence if you read this.

We have been hurting, but above all we must have Hope.   I shall now walk back into the clouds of the Big Sky."

Elvis Has Finally Found Peace

A Hunk of Astral Love who is always near, Elvis has found his voice once again:

"Now, this ain't the first time I've communicated to y'all from over here. My spirit is bound up with your popular culture. As long as you believe in me, part of me will always be there.

Livin' with a one word name is both difficult and rewarding. 'You are the Elvis' people would say. Bangin' chicks and makin' flicks….doing lots and lots of drugs…

Shit…this kid translatin' is great. He'll write anything I transmit. Other psychics always watered me down….all the friggin' bastards were trying to steal a piece of me, but I'm Elvis baby…you gotta know that I am ready to Rock N Roll.

My first show over here was not much different from my last one over there. I got lit up, put on a hip suit, batted my eyelashes and sang, 'Love me tender…..'

Gotta put in a word for my little baby doll Lisa

Marie. Keep away from that freak, baby. You know who I mean. Oh how your daddy loves you. That Cage guy, now he's cool.

Boy you Americans have gotten crazier than old Elvis himself. You wouldn't even notice me now. I am much better to you as a legend. I started the faster/fatter trend and you all followed me off the cliff. Nobody cares what happens to the insides.

Militarily, you gotta watch out for the Chinese. You don't think someone who has traveled as much as The King would be out of the geopolitical loop do you? This is a fine part of the Super Channeling method offered by the Facilitator. I just feel it and he makes it happen; sweet luxury in modern astral communication. They are weakening the US now with currency and flooding the market with cheap goods. Standing by waiting to strike the death blow, they figure, 'why waste time and treasure, while you are self destructing?' Keep your eyes open friends.

Priscilla, you were always my jewel. Thank God we had some good times before it was too late. Your beauty is of the stars.

Please remember me for more than jumpsuits and

cheesy tunes. Most of all, I was and am always being me. I went for life and made some mistakes, but that's okay. I still do about a show per Earth week on our transportable light stages. Besides that, I study with Sri Yukteswar and meditate. Thank you for listening. Elvis has finally found peace. "

Herr Mozart Takes Us Farther

"Though you buried me in an unmarked grave I'll come forward and clear up a few things for the good of humanity. We cornerstones of history are very sensitive to heritage being disregarded in the modern era. Building upon the aesthetic of our lineage we tried to most perfectly translate spirit into the form of the epoch.

My gifted youth was partially due to the fact that in my previous incarnation I was the composer known as Palestrina. I had perfected the art of simple melodic brilliance and had found deep harmony in the spirit. Much has been made in small circles of our transparent similarities.

Your movie Amadeus was indeed entertaining, but much more dramatic than the day to day sufferings of real life that I underwent. Remember to honor your artists while they are alive. They don't need to wallow in the mud to express their inspiration. They give the society's soul wings. This is something that Western Civilization is once again desperately missing.

The Facilitator of this message has an interesting idea with the Transcendence World Movement.

Following in the footsteps of the Renaissance and the European Enlightenment of which I was a part, the beauty of humanity once again rises above the bounds of misaligned views and conceptual irregularities. The artist becomes leader of culture instead of the politician.

One thing I beseech you to do is take another look at the work of Nannerl my sister. She was simply brilliant! When I would come home after another long night of Piano Concertos, she would be secretly working out her own sweet dreams into realizations. She would praise me and I would say, "Someday you will be seen as the true genius of the family." There are several of her masterworks that are yet to be discovered.

Our father knew that a woman would not be able to produce as much money as a man, so he chose to ride me like a dog. If I had to do it all again I wouldn't have deferred so much of my own wishes to Old Leo. The bastard was so full of himself that he never allowed for the freedom of movement I desperately needed. I eventually died of his suffocation. My Requiem was as much for my unreturned love for him (Trombone Solo theme) as it was for my Earth departure (Dies Irae).

Super Channelings

Salieri was not quite a maniacal murderer; he was much too mediocre for that. Just imagine an uptight librarian who is terribly troubled if so much as a single book is out of place. Such a man might find some order, but never inspiration.

I still give concerts semi-regularly over here. The Plato Amphitorium is quite a magnificent venue. Beethoven and Haydn brought 1001 young musicians to hear my new work "Symphony of Saint's Songs", and I could just barely make out the group amidst the backdrop of souls. The work is a combination Opera and Symphony with Astral tunes used for themes much in the manner folk tunes were used in Nationalistic music of the 1800s.

It has been pleasant to use the mind of the writer to convey a few things I felt unresolved about. Although part of me has reincarnated several times already, part of me has remained ever your Herr Mozart."

Marilyn Monroe Ends Her Torment

"I have been dying to get through to the Facilitator for at least 3 days. I keep coming into his energy field and revealing what I have to say, but he has held me off, working on other things. Finally he has the time and space for me to get my emotion cleared.

This is something I have attempted with other psychics, but so often they brings some of themselves to the reading and filter out what might seem offensive to some. I know this Facilitator doesn't sensor and if anything can express my intention better than I could myself. I believe he calls this process Super Channeling.

There have been some gross misunderstandings about me, the era in which I lived, and my relationship with the president. JFK was the real thing. At the time, we all had such a history making feeling. John was going to lead us towards the potential that so many have actively sought to thwart. I was not simply his concubine. In fact we had many sweet and meaningful talks. I was willing to be somewhat subservient because I understood the magnitude of the circumstance.

At first you could call our relationship a fling, but we definitely grew bonds that became difficult for us both. We wanted to be together more than was possible and we both suffered for it. Hanging around with Frankie and Robbie, John hardened up us he had to in order to maintain integrity in leading the free world.

How could one justify being self-absorbed when we were standing off with the Russians and planning on going to the moon? John told me that his most lasting legacy would be to restore the money to the people of the USA. He said that this had to be done very carefully because there were enemies all around. I didn't fully understand this, but could sense that he felt this was a very dangerous thing to do.

On another note, I have no idea how you in your world can still think of me as a SEX symbol after all of this time (especially with the images you ingest these days). Don't be surprised if you find more of your beautiful young women ending up dead of a broken heart. I really just wanted to be Norma Jean and dreamed of living in a small home on a small farm with a man who loved me for me. The big screen image of the Starlet Marilyn made me larger than life and pretty much unapproachable.

I appreciate Joe's personal vigilance after the end. He was a good man with a small mind. We were friends and our relationship, though a mixed-bag, was one thing in life that was tangible. Elton and I were special friends in a past life which is why he feels our connection so strongly yet inexplicably. He is a beautiful person and I am grateful that he felt called to honor me with his music. In a way he was invoking my spirit and conveyed much more the truth of my being than your decadent mass media ever could.

The popular impression of me is so far removed from the reality of my soul being that I will be able to move on now that I have released a bit of vitriol. We all must make do with things less perfect than we might like. It is okay. Next go around, I will do a better job of accepting my circumstance and allowing my own Will to express itself no matter what. Your Earth is magnificent and life is fleeting. Make the most of it.

Love to you,
Marilyn"

The Ancient Greek Writer Homer Returns

Homer describes the aftermath of Troy's downfall and further illustrates under-recognized events and ideas from the Ancient Classical Era:

"The Iliad told of the Trojan War's last year, and the Odyssey of the journey home of he who was inspired by Athena to concoct the bloody ruse that ended King Priam's once mighty and glorious city. Odysseus's voyage navigating Poseidon's treacherous kingdom, was representative of the secrets of emotional transformation inscribed as a mystical adventure. This second of my Epics was to prepare the reader for the third which has thus far been lost to human history. In it was encoded the deepest of the Ancient World's sacred truths.

Much after my time, Virgil's exploration of the wanderings of Aeneas (the second greatest Trojan warrior on his way to found Rome) was the closest thing to the spirit of my writings and should be included in any Classical Education. Dante spoke effectively of Hell's Inferno and our pre-Christian mythology as recorded by Ovid remains a testament (though shallow when stripped of its symbolic meaning), to the ability of the Classical World to probe deeper into the layers of life.

The philosophers Socrates and Pythagorus embodied these ideals in their esoteric teachings, some of which have also been temporarily lost. Many works of theatre such as those by Sophocles, Aeschylus, and Euripides along with the few remaining scraps of written music as recorded by Gregoria Paniagua evoke the aesthetic most accurately portrayed by the pottery which you display in your modern museums.

Zeus himself remains available to those who would seek his advice. Even now he tells me to say unto you, 'Though you have made your Lincoln into my image, know that it is I who am the inspiration. Those of you who are not confused by the reassigning of archetypal labels will intuitively know that I am a master schooled in the art of soul retrieval. Chosen to lead the other healers of light, I had the combination of Strength and Wisdom necessary to hold back the Titans of Darkness. Cronus had bastardized the transcendent teachings of Grandfather Uranus and turned them into some crazy dogma unrecognizable as anything but rule by force. His general Atlas is still being punished for his foolish attempt to stamp out the rule of truth.'

My Third Epic 'The Oracle' was written from the perspective of the Delphic Oracle as she tells the tale of Mercury flying over the burning ruins of Troy. There are references to Odysseus, Achilles, Hector, and Aeneas, but the focus is on Paris's Heart as it comes to grips with the ramifications of desire's indulgence in the moment of his death. There are many asides, including the death of both warriors Ajax, and Cassandra's manipulations of Agamemnon.

To the people of your time I say but one thing: Seek to know thyself and seek to share what you find. You can not be convinced of lies if you live the truth. Often in the affairs of humanity, nefarious groups have come together to perpetuate philosophy that flies in the face of principle and the common good. In these times, the bold speak louder and the heroic wax poetic.

The Dream of Divine Humanity on Earth is not lost. Body-Mind-Spirit must be balanced to allow essence to come forth. Invigorate your own past and create newly brilliant conceptions in the present. It is glorious to speak once more and to do so through a conduit who shares my lofty ideals and sensitivity to detail. The Muses have blessed him and much like the Delphic Priestess, he is capable of revealing whatever he turns his attention to, whenever he intends it."

Thomas Jefferson Comes Out of Retirement to Save the Republic

"At last I have found a conduit capable of delivering a message with the style of elegance and grace with which I am accustomed to communicating. One cannot deliver a cold and simple discourse to explain the intricacies of philosophy. Nor can the small minded individual appropriately comprehend the matters of history that are not concrete, but ever-changing.

Again and again your politicians refer to the sacred cow of the Founding Fathers in a manner of deification that implies argument is not to follow. As if we all believed the same thing and that which we believed was static! Nothing could be further from the truth as politics has always been a messy and evolving sport. Even from the beginning of the Republic there were those ready to betray her at the slightest provocation.

Using the technique of arresting debate by preying upon fears, baser minds have been able to temporarily gain the upper hand. There would be no reason for me to come forward thusly if a statesman of my caliber was doing this service in the land of the living. Due to the void of leadership and the danger of our dream falling into disrepair, I have stepped into the light once more to give sense to those who respond to such things.

America was founded on the Mystical. As the children of the European Enlightenment, we were to be as Gods on Earth reflecting the Glory of Creation. Our inner circle understood things that many of you are just now coming into possession of as knowledge. To clear up a gravely mistaken point of conjecture, we were not referring to a Christian God of limited dogmatic leanings. We decided to use simply the term GOD, because this translates in every language as the Individual's concept of a Higher Power. It was the perfect choice and the consensus of the writers because of its simplicity and universality. This devolved as lesser men, knowing not the mystery behind the form, applied their own meaning and claimed it was our intent.

Oh how your destiny might have sprung forth a divergent stream had John F. Kennedy been granted a longer life! His path to the sacred was not unlike my own as he had a keen mind and mastery over himself as a decision maker. Getting to a point within where all choices and ramifications were seen on a continuum of possibilities partly ruled by chance and partly upon creative manifestation, he was ready to lead an American Renaissance. Historically, focus intensely on the months prior to his death. These are things to be recovered and magnified today.

As the Solar System vibration circumstance has changed dramatically, new methods of governing will have to be instigated. There will be an initial resistance that must be overcome. The evil beings responsible for the delay of an Enlightened Republic, are able to do so because they are protected by a cloak of magic from their astral plane manipulators. Each one of you can rise above this, but it will take great determination, stamina, and imagination; characteristics of the American Spirit.

On a personal note, please stop slandering my memory in the ways that are of your time. I am dead and gone friends. My love affairs and whims were signs only that I was human. I served higher principles as good as any man. I devoted my life to the dream of a better world for us all. You can still succeed if each noble soul takes personal responsibility for making a difference."

John Lennon Clears the Air

"It's about time you take my message. I've been trying to get through for days. You'll take Thomas Jefferson, but you leave one of your favorite inspirations waiting at the doorstep. I know. I know. You are creating so I will let it go.

I am frenetic and adamant in one proclamation. No one speaks in my name. You must not believe that Yoko is expressing my voice. By now if allowed to live my full life plan I would have made up quietly with Paul. We both would have put the past to rest and accepted each other. We had divergent streams that were meant to run back together. Perhaps we would have secretly recorded some tracks and left them for humanity after we died. It would have been my idea, but Paul would have loved it.

To my son Julian I have to say you have some reason to be bitter, but don't let it rule your feelings of me. Discover me the way others do, not in the limited man, but in the inspiration he allowed to come through. It is time to heal and grow up. You weren't meant to be a singer. Find your true joy and you'll find peace.

Sean, escape the totalitarian thought influence of your mother. She used to be lighter, but life has been hard for her. She is associated with loss and it has worn on her very much. A type of Jackie O., she is obligated by society to play the role of a moment frozen in time. I have never forgotten our joyous times together.

Over here, I still write songs and perform at my leisure. Continuing work on developing my consciousness, I have re-discovered the deep beauty of brother George. It is a wonder we didn't foster his aspect of the Beatles a bit more. Perhaps it would have balanced the situation. Ringo's childishness didn't help. If you doubt it, feel for the substance behind his words and you'll come up with thin air. I loved them all in their own way, but I can't be associated with solely these lads forever.

After my arrival in the astral realm I tended bar to get grounded. At first I was furious at my death because there were some things at the time only I could do, and I was the rare person who followed through. Looking from over here and assessing the situation it was the bloody politics that did me in. I must say I never saw it coming. It was definitely a hit, not just some crazy fan, and you are a fool if you believe that story. It is the same type of recycled BS used to cover-up all kinds of crimes.

Lately, I've taken to painting more often. This would have happened in my Earth life if I had lived longer. Perhaps I would be more like your own Cosmic Bloggers who take up the Love mission we got started in the '60s. Don't ever for a second believe the battle is lost. You are going to make it. There is much help coming from this side. Part of the point of pain is to liberate you.

Now get back to work and tell your mother you love her."

Elephant Oversoul: Love all Creatures

"In some cultures I am known as Ganesh, but that is merely one subset of the possibilities of perception. These parameters were formalized by one culture and are colored by the influences therein. Once an idea hangs around Earth for long enough, humans tend to adopt a default brain pattern. As we continue this transmission, remove the mental barriers and see again my true brilliance. I am the one mythological reality behind the many incarnated elephants.

Representing not just the acts of animals, but the symbolic qualities intrinsic to species and form, it is time to clear the air and make healing possible. When you see one of my images raging across the land and exuding hostility towards humanity, remove the snap judgment in your mind and look deeply into the truth of it. We are a very collective sort with long developed capabilities of love and empathy. When one of us is hurt, we are all hurt. Can you even begin to imagine the suffering we have incurred in the last couple of hundred years?

Even in the days when we were leading armies, we felt we had a place and a purpose. Today we are discarded as if worth nothing more than a few pieces of paper holding the faces of butchers from the past. Many of you when confronted directly with film or pictures of us being slaughtered feel it is wrong, but blame only the one doing the killing. Are not the people behind the decisions which create the circumstance for this atrocity to flourish responsible in some way? How about the one who looks away, does nothing, and wraps themselves up in a blanket of distraction instead of resisting entropy?

There have been times when we have attempted to get your attention. Displays of unity and consciousness have been repeatedly made, but again and again you reference only your limited preconceptions and fail to see that we operate on a different frequency than you do. At last I have found a vehicle for expression through a kindly universal human who has it in him to take personal responsibility for bringing powerful change through profound understanding. I thank him and thank you for taking the time to listen to our unexpressed Will. In this greater environment of planetary ascension, it is at last possible for us to resolve the discrepancy between us.

We do not belong in zoos any more than the other trapped members of the animal kingdom. Injured animals that have been restored and could no longer exist in the wild may be enjoyed in the manner of some of your more progressive establishments who through good sense and personal honor create very pleasant environments which make for a better life than none at all. We need to have the space to feel free. A small reserve that gets smaller and is constantly invaded by unchallenged rule breakers is not a proper place. Then we are blamed by villages when seeking food for our young!

Your kind and ours have had an unsteady relationship since the days of the wooly mammoth and Cro-Magnon man. We do not seek to be worshipped; we are offering friendship. Learn our language and through that bridge we can become more familiar with yours. On equal footing, we will not have a grievance which disturbs the tranquility that brings peace between beings. Please consider deeply what I have described and any individual who feels this to be true, send us Love. We will connect and over the years we can move closer and closer to sharing our Earth with each other and all of God's creatures."

Angel Buddha Christopher

Angel Buddha Christopher on God and Creation

Even as I reach out Now, I am connected to God. For those who react as if it is preposterous, I respond that it is more unbelievable that you are not. How dare anyone proclaim as off-limits the missing link! Things have changed and they will continue to change.

Those afraid of even the slightest provocation towards conflict tend to freak out over any little thing. Nobody benefits from such a weak position. Scared to make a peep on their own behalf, they wonder why nobody understands them.

There are layers upon layers of experience to uncover. Every dream and vision happens always. Luckily God is hipper than most realize. He says in my ear, "Oooooo, I am sooo scary," as He giggles and makes ooga booga hands. C'mon and finish this. It isn't so hard. Once you see, you will know why the message had to be transmitted this way.

Christ just stepped forward through the Father to remind us all that we are equal Sons and

Daughters of God. The Holy Spirit is the Mother and the Soul of the Earth. Each of us is 1/3 of the Trinity. Although there are many individuals, the process only unfolds in the One and each time it is the expression of the Whole. Celebration vibrates to the Far Corners while our minds absorb the raining starlight.

God is aware of W., Chirac, Blair, Sharon, Condi, Rummy, and Cheney etc… Actually He says, "You have to admit there is a kind of beauty in Cheney; so perfectly he plays the scoundrel. I wish I could help the Anger which keeps arresting his Heart. Deep inside he wants to die and take everybody with him. This will not be allowed." Some of the others are like character actors in an old play. The new world comes when those of you who are self-conscious organize in a different way. Do this by recognizing each other and following higher ideals.

Buddha is not actively involved here. He simply waits for the dust to settle. Like a lighthouse he still shines through the fog to those who wish to travel to him. The 'Babaji to Yogananda' line of Masters continues to gently but firmly guide evolution of emerging souls. Osho will pop right in if you let your guard down. Watch out, he

Angel Buddha Christopher
may be looking for you. Barry Long is gone, but
has left behind tremendously beneficial maps for
the journey.

Angels are working closely with those called to
transmit the message of awakening over the
internet. Some of the fairy folk emerge in the
darkest part of the night to do what they can
around the fringes of human society. They look
after plants and encourage lightness of mood.
Over a long period of time, their contribution
adds up, making a big difference to the default
state of mind.

Of course entities such as Bigfoot, the Loch Ness
Monster, and Pteradactyls exist in the astral
realm. Occasionally, their world and ours blend
together, and we share space. It is no harm at all
and certainly nothing to be concerned about. It is
a beauty like Giraffes, Elephants, Hippos and
Rhinos.

Within every cell of every creature lives the
unifying presence. In that place, there is no
distinction of form. Primordial goo beats the
rhythm of Creation.

Angel Buddha Christopher: You Are Not Alone

Early in the process, each has to invent one's own path out of the darkness. It is a necessary circumstance. The empowering satisfaction of growth can only come when you decide to move alone. This is not to say the burgeoning Soul is helpless. There are facilitating indicators secretly planted all around by loving beings. The work that awaits you when crossing over the threshold is precisely of this kind. Seeing the struggling buds of hope, you will throw information fertilizer over the grounds to nurture nature.

From within the vines we see the chaos, from without, the order. Even war has its own cosmic role to play. We will awaken when we have suffered enough to be finished with it. Erasing brain grooves that seek a pain fix, we shift our energies to higher parts of the mind. Every being has this potential. Can we begin to fathom the tragedy of one who comes and goes, never finding this treasure? Some speculate that this is their choice/path and how Free Will plays itself out. But what if Life never got a chance?

Children rarely emerge unscathed from a development which includes sometimes contradictory rules both spoken and unspoken relentlessly pounded into their head. How confusing to see that the gatekeepers often do not follow their own muddled instructions and the motivating machinations underneath tend to revolve around control. How can the innocent Love when their vulnerability is turned against them? They become hard and substitute the false for the real in efforts to find approval from their world so they can survive.

This intricate damage must be undone. I know some whose eyes fall upon these words have aching souls and that is precisely why it flows out to you. Otherwise there would be nothing to say, and we all would be laughing and loving in this realm and the next. That day will arrive eventually. It can happen for you NOW! Find friendship with the divine energy. God created the Universe so you can create your Life.

Oh my lovelies, I do weep for you on occasion. Sometimes I poke at the bubbles of illusion and see how disoriented you become. Gently I whisper in your ear sweet truths, and when you are not looking, I put happy pictures in your background. One day this accumulation of

Angel Buddha Christopher

Giving from all Service oriented beings will saturate and Love will be everywhere on the outside as it is on the inside of Existence.

Consider the animals who have always been your friends. To kill majestic creatures for encroaching on human territory as many city governments do, is a crime the Lord is concerned about. He could interfere, but then the whole experiment would be over. It is for YOU to interfere. Can you not understand that Life is Life and it is simply poor planning that causes these interspecies misunderstandings? You have had scientists and mystics explain this to you in a myriad of ways. How can we reach you and heal this scar? Maybe your weather would calm down if you would figure out some of these disturbances swirling in your collective psyche.

There are many among you who every day produce artifacts of transformation designed to uplift those living now and in the future. Often the people at large keep their back turned so as not to have the difficulty of being exposed to something which will disturb their slumber. Misers live in mansions and the godly often keep shop in a basement. This must be turned around. God's vessels should at least be afforded a healthy home.

In the skies just beyond our eyes are angels, often working with legions of people devoted to relaying their messages. Surely one must discern what rings true to their heart, but one must not be so scrutinizing as to critique themselves straight to an early grave with an empty life resume. Openness is essential for the light to shine through the window. Honor those among you who present the unusual in a magnificent manner. Their work is noted in the Annals of History and the Halls of the Akashic Records. I know our own translator of this message holds a hope that his various verbal lectures were recorded in this way. He is a crazy person whose main concern about dying is whether his collected works will be attended to on the astral plane.

No thing that has ever been, is, or ever will be, disappears completely. There will always be an imprint of its existence. If a tree falls in the forest and there is nobody there to hear it, it does not preclude the possibility that one day someone might arrive with the subtle ability to pick up the remaining echoes. If something occurs, there is no need to philosophize about the perceiver. Is it not the expression of the Creator none-the-less? As those of you with journals of your most

Angel Buddha Christopher
precious thoughts know, there is a sublime
beauty in something that is solely your very own.

Trust that there are others who understand, and
they will find you. They are waiting patiently for
the magnetism to take over and bring you close.
Enjoy talking about the wonders of the galaxy.
There is nothing to the myth of modern times.
Truth has always been the same. Humanity is
finally ready to accept it on a larger scale. Be
patient with the process and steadfast in your
devotion and success is guaranteed.

Good fortune in your endeavors.

Angel Buddha Christopher: Sail to the Stars in Love

Can it be but with grace and elegance that one sings of the Love in the Universe? Everywhere pulsing with Joy, the intrinsic beat of nature's rhythm squeezes every last bit of Life out of every single continuous moment to moment transition. There is no stopping Here and if you try, you will have no choice but to make up for lost time. Initially doing double duty just to stay afloat, the transcending humans eventually catch up with themselves and can ride the wave of glory to eternity.

Understanding beyond limitation is within reach for any who can Love themselves enough to accept the whole Truth. This is the essential lesson permeating all of the dramatic events unfolding upon the Earth. The scary darkness is merely a by-product of the emergence of a whole new realm. The horrors of war and the corruption of man vs. man has always been as ugly as it is today, only we are seeing it more clearly now. There is no way for this remaining past to ever rectify itself within its own subset of parameters.

Occasionally brave souls have openly expressed the Love within their hearts in efforts to share the golden pathway to God. It would be hard not to tell a friend that the most magnificent thing that has ever happened continues to happen. There is no color, pitch, texture, scent, or delicacy which can do any more but open the door. Through the gateway there is brilliant fluidity which defies explanation other than to bathe in its healing energies.

Consider not meditation an obligation and begin approaching yourself with Love and acceptance. Allow relaxation to take over and release the thought knots/nots which use up your energy on an ongoing basis. Do not blame the butcher for giving you a rotten slab of beef and anger over injustice will subside. Sorrow is there to be fully expressed and finished. Holding back complicates the matter into something far more difficult. Tears of pain become tears of Joy when Light shines into the lonely shadow filled corners.

Cowards never begin while a hero's Love stays the course. Each will get what is their due based on the choices they have made in crucial situations. Anything hidden is revealed as it is by the vibration which sustains all things. You can not keep secrets from the all-pervasive presence.

Angel Buddha Christopher

This is not to say there is judgment. All will simply be laid transparent on the way. For some this will be thrust upon them after death in the Bardo. For those who willingly discovered the truth while on Earth, they will sail out of the body to the stars.

Angel Buddha Christopher: Children of a Conscious Universe

Tuning in to the highest Source, harmony establishes a flow that cascades like a mighty waterfall off an enormous cliff. The water vapor dances with the Sun creating rainbows wherever you look. Leaping over and through the light are fairies you can almost see through. When you become aware of them, they become aware of you. There is nothing as beautiful as a silent knowing between two beings of different realms who have found a way to connect. A rare pleasure, this opportunity is becoming available to more people as understanding compounds and the collective lifts its vibration.

When you finally stop seeking an end, the details become easier to deal with. Sometimes the every day moments of sharing time with someone you love take on more brilliance. Newness in the now of life adds the spark from within that twinkles in the imagination and encourages the heart to expand to the far corners of the Earth. Such wonderful and gracious support from the Conscious Universe comes to any person sensible enough to realize that it is possible. One can surround themselves with a cloud of darkness if

117

they choose to do so, but they must no longer seek to spread it to the children of the light.

You skeptical minded yet loving hearted humans had better learn to put the horse in front of the cart. Dismantling your own chance of salvation is certainly not the wisest course of action. It is good to scrutinize the fluff, but when the monumental comes across your path, be kind enough to allow yourself the time to consider it. Sometimes there is a delay between exposure and recognition. Capacity to sink into the frequency of a vibe depends upon the nature of your alignment, and the remaining thought patterns which color experience. In the crack between worlds a hand can be reached that a Soul can grab in friendship and determination.

There is a call beyond it all that echoes throughout eternity. Once you get to the end of your rope, it is the right moment to climb on back. Swinging there waiting for death, some forget where they have come from. Do not abdicate your divine throne over a few worldly tricks. Shake the cobwebs and return your mission to what matters. Every fear creates the object of its dread. No matter what the circumstance, the best choice is to radiate your own good energy and construct blessed thought forms. Beware of that which seeks to control your state of mind. Observe the aggressive input from a distance and remain centered.

Beloved star people, the truth is so close to you. There is no distance. Just like a yawn, you are constantly cleansed of all unrighteousness. Holy is the kingdom you live in. Clear out your associations and see the truth of it: Holy is the kingdom you live in. To spell it out, your very residence is not as solid as you believe. There is a celebration going on right below the surface. You can scowl, but that will just make us all laugh at the funny stories we can share when you get back here. Humming beneath your feet is a universal equation that forms shapes which grow life. Blossoming in your chest is the One Heart.

Angel Buddha Christopher: Love of Earth's Vibration

If I could leap inside your mind and explode into a billion light beams I would do so this instant. In lieu of such a dangerously invasive maneuver, I will do my best to explain as many intricate details of the astral tapestry as possible. Expressing in ways that if you go along will turn into realms in the imagination, I open the floodgates and become a portal for the universe to flow through. Gently but firmly I lift you.

Fear not loved ones as you all indeed are and always will be a part of the Father. Always and forever will the Cosmic Mother be available to nurture you in the ways she did through the women you have known in your life. Your brothers and sisters the stars, reflect light back and forth to reveal an invisible but perceivable web that tells the hidden history of your journey. Very few of you are native Earthians. Perhaps 1 in 10 grew up from Gaia's mud. The rest of you have origins from all areas of Heaven and the Universe.

That is what the blue-green planet, 3rd body out from the center of your solar system is currently committed to seeing through. Offering herself as a resting place for weary souls, the tough Love of Earth's vibrations will either burn the impurities or finish you once and for all. Although no thing disappears in this existence, forms can change and fragment to such a point to where they are unrecognizable. Either you unify and disperse consciously into the Universe or entropy scatters you until you are no more.

If you are seeing this right now, there is no need of concern as you are meant to learn the truth. The only question is whether or not you will do your part. If your mind is gibbering about channeling doubts and hesitations due to your current reality you only need consider what happens of its own accord. What does it matter where a message is from if it stirs your heart? Why hesitate when there is nothing to lose? One must dive into life and swim the churning seas boldly to arrive at the destination that always changes.

So many collect bits and pieces of knowledge and then parade around as if they know the final answer. This betrays their unknowing because there is no conclusion that suddenly lifts the seeker from seeking to bliss. This is what Buddha discovered under the bodhi tree. It isn't until

Angel Buddha Christopher

you've looked under every stone that you know
for yourself that this is the case. Perhaps trust
could save you time, but it cannot be false. The
autobahn to heaven is driven by those who resist
not. Opening the hollow bamboo, Truth itself
takes root from the inside and becomes your
personal chauffeur.

It is a joy to be here with you. I am with you even
as you read this.

Angel Buddha Christopher: Heaven on Earth

Cast your eyes away from images of horror. Your life is shaped by what you spend time focusing your attention on. It is entirely possible to create a pocket of Heaven even in the depths of Hell. If you are lucky enough to become a syntropic force, you will find that the cracked dirt of Hell just needed a little water. There will always be places out of reach, and they are needed for the deep grounding of 3D incarnation. There will always be reds and violets to hold the oranges, yellows, greens, blues, and indigos of the world.

The children of indigo are simply children born with their third eye open. Anyone can gain the ability to read the history of the Universe directly from the Source itself as these enchanted ones do. There are no exclusive clubs and scattered dispersion of psychic abilities. With practice, we all have so many talents that we will be more than fulfilled through the expression of our creative love/life force. Focus your attention in the middle of your forehead anytime you wish to retrieve information.

Deeper and deeper into your forehead… Your 6th chakra will give you a completely new and brilliant view of your place in existence. The falling star is falling for you. The frog king reigns over the pond so that you might sit by the side of it and listen to the frog people's songs. All animals are representatives of a whole kingdom. Ambassadors to the human race, they willingly take slaughter just to have the opportunity to interact with you. They care about you and the human species could communicate with all of them so much better.

No human has a right or a need to bend any other to his/her Will. Wills can align and a strong Will can lift the undeveloped Will of one who resonates with the frequency that reveals their own potential. A true leader leaves you feeling empowered and more confident to carry out your own life of possibilities. The living master, aligned with the Universe becomes a gateway through which you can see/feel the mystery firsthand. This is a rare occasion not to be taken for granted. One who hears the ringing of the bell should jump up and take action now! There may not be a chance like this for many lifetimes. You are alive. You are here and recognize truth.

Dive into the possibilities. When Jesus said, "Come and I will make you fishers of men," the

receptive brothers dropped their nets and walked
in the present to a whole new future. No longer
simple people in a limited role mini-series, they
became witnesses of the beyond. Resonating with
light, they too moved into the world. In years,
the contagious wave spread across the globe.
This has happened many times in many ways.
Even as each holy message flows, it also has to
ebb one day. There will be a new version of the
truth made available by spirit conduits to meet
the needs of any given time.

Do not think that free play is without its own type
of order. Too many linear thinkers have already
done too much damage. Consider these words
like raindrops bouncing off your DNA. Playing
the codes like a keyboard, some of you will light
up like a Christmas tree. Suddenly knowledge
will reveal itself to you and you will get your
mission. Read it clearly and do not hesitate or
you might miss the sacred train.

Mission of the Creative Cosmos

To invoke the unity of Eastern Wisdom and Western Art.

To assist in the evolving consciousness and destiny of humanity.

To make this information available to the widest possible audience.

http://www.creativecosmos.org

www.ingramcontent.com/pod-product-compliance
Lightning Source LLC
Chambersburg PA
CBHW072022040426
42447CB00009B/1699